FAITH,  FLINT & FOC

G000153716

To give love like that, no questions asked,
We don't realise: Christ is generosity untold.

Bill Smith, St Luke's Church

Detail of east window, stained glass, St Luke's Church

ACKNOWLEDGEMENTS

St Luke's Queen's Park Press gratefully acknowledges the financial assistance of Diocese of Chichester Mission Fund, Westhill Endowment Fund, AllChurches Trust/E.I.G., Brighton & Hove Bus and Coach Company, Christopher Stringer Funeral Directors, The Independent, Basil and Olive McDonald, Elizabeth Wicks and funders who wish to remain anonymous.

Copyright © 2015 St Luke's Queen's Park Press and the authors

Faith, Flint & Footstep – St Luke's Church, Queen's Park: community arts and heritage

All rights reserved. No part of this publication may be reproduced without written permission, except in the case of brief extracts embodied in articles, reviews or lectures.

British Library Catalogue in Publication Data
A catalogue record for this book is available from the British Library
ISBN 978-0-9934041-0-8

First published in Great Britain in 2015 by St Luke's Queen's Park Press, Brighton, UK

Typeset by Woking Print & Publicity

Designer Richard Woods

Managing Editor The Revd Julie Newson

Editor Evlynn Sharp

Photography Ashen Venema and Evlynn Sharp

Musical Director Chris Whitley-Jones

Audio production Adliberate

CD duplication CopyDog, Brighton

Additional images Chris Lowe, Lisa Holdcroft and The Regency Society

Printed and bound by Woking Print & Publicity,
The Print Works, St John's Lye, Woking, Surrey GU21 1RS
Tel: 01483 884884

Numbers in italics refer to pages in which images appear:
Ashen Venema, 6, 10, 11, 13, 14, 18, 19, 21, 22 (angels), 24, 25, 29, 35, 38, 40, 46, 47 (portrait), 48, 52 (trowel), 56 (flint)
Evlynn Sharp, inside title page, 4, 5, 7, 8, 12, 15, 16, 17, 20, 22 (angel), 23, 26, 27, 28, 30, 31, 32, 33, 36, 37, 39, 41, 42, 43, 44, 45, 47 (music), 49, 50, 54, 56 (church), 58, 59, 60 (stone), 61, 63 (Pepper Pot, garden temple), 64 (writing; bus; Delilah; Post Office; store)

Writing, images and music by kind permission of authors, photographers and musicians where possible. Copyright disclaimer: St Luke's Church, Queen's Park, has made all reasonable efforts to ensure that the reproduction of content in this publication is done with the full consent of copyright holders. If you feel that your copyright has not been fully respected, please contact us by email: julie.newson@btinternet.com

St Luke's Church, Queen's Park, Brighton, holds services on Sunday at 10am and on Wednesday at 9.30am. For further information please visit the website: www.stlukeschurchbrighton.webeden.co.uk/
Deacon in Charge The Revd Julie Newson. Tel: 01273 570978
Registered Charity number: 1154483

CONTENTS

Angel, stained glass, east window, St Luke's Church

FOREWORD

Faith, Flint & Footstep reveals the potential of socially-engaged ministry with inclusivity and accessibility at the core. It reflects the aim of Julie Newson – the Deacon in Charge of St Luke's Church – to strengthen goodwill and creative self-expression among people of all ages and diversities in the community.

Contributors to the book range from children under five years old to senior citizens of 90 plus. Across the generations, we see there are common interests, values and shared experiences connecting us in many ways from faith to forgiveness, tears to silence, bereavement to hope.

We can also see how the local community is a mirror of national and global concerns such as matters of war and peace. Each individual's reflection travels beyond spatial boundaries and reminds us we are witnesses of life through its joys, grief and challenges as gradually we build a history of ourselves.

This book presents archival material that sheds light on our present-day world so helping us to make a bridge between past, present and future. The unbroken span of time exemplifies our part in the narrative of life, and our wholeness.

The heritage chapter mentions women in the medical profession, and it makes me think about how my life links to the lives of these pioneers from whom emancipation is forged.

Faith, Flint & Footstep weaves together themes of heritage and everyday realities through the traditions, purposes and circumstances of people who are linked by bonds of place and potential. The voices of people in community call to us here and give an achievement to celebrate, a step for the future.

Rose Turner

Dr Rose Turner FRCP
Consultant in Palliative Medicine
Martlets Hospice, Hove
Sussex Community NHS Trust, Brighton General Hospital
October 2015

INTRODUCTION

What defines St Luke's Church, Queen's Park, is a ministry of welcome, a love of community, and a strong rootedness in the source of this love. Deacon in Charge Julie Newson along with the church's poet in residence Evlynn Sharp spent time working in the heart of community to make this book, *Faith, Flint & Footstep*. The words and images here remind us our collective and personal histories offer greater awareness of the past, a sense of completeness in the present and inspiration for the future.

Faith, Flint & Footstep arises from the commitment by members of St Luke's to arts, heritage and social projects in the parish. During this book project, archive materials such as nineteenth-century communion records and music books began to resurface from forgotten corners of the church. This material provides a glimpse into the past and is evidence of the faith of past generations.

Processional Cross, St Luke's Church

Historian Louise Peskett draws together heritage threads and depicts the growth of the church within the community. Little-known facts emerge of the circumstances of local people's lives in the nineteenth century such as pioneering women in the medical profession, and realities of the workhouse at Brighton General Hospital. Yet *Faith, Flint & Footstep* also steers our attention towards the present day, and the enthusiasm of people across all diversities, ages and abilities to introduce us to their thoughts and feelings about life.

Deacon Julie and Evlynn put together creative writing workshops involving people everywhere. From pop-up, write-a-poem-and-prayer events – by the busy Pepper Pot bus stop opposite the church and at Brighton General Hospital – to work with the Sunday School children and those attending the Crafty Kids Cook Club in the church's community space. From visiting people in their flats and in care homes – to hear of special memories – to visiting local hostelries and encouraging people to write.

Initiatives with the local St Luke's Primary School and dialogue with St John's School and College point up the creative imagination as the connective bridge between us all through times and locations.

Creative writing workshops in the vicarage and the church itself put people's attention to themes such as bereavement, place and time. The key topics such as forgiveness that engage people at a local level are highly pertinent to the wider community.

In *Faith, Flint & Footstep*, Marina Cantacuzino who is founder of The Forgiveness Project charity offers insight into the specific task of forgiving.

From its early days, St Luke's has had fantastic choirs offering music to touch the spirit. In this book, Music Director Chris Whitley-Jones provides a background to his work with the choir in today's world and the consistent high standards necessary to bring the best of church music to the community.

Within the church, there is a link of three ordained women who speak candidly in *Faith, Flint & Footstep* about their experiences amidst changing views that support their faith activities. Russell Robinson who has been attending the church from boyhood into manhood mentions his thoughts about women's ordination and presents his faith perspectives. This writing is very real and empowering of transformation of attitudes and silences.

The weaving of poetry, prayer and silence inspires Fr Michael Forrest's thoughtful words, and Fr Steven Foster shows his feeling for a ministry that honours senior citizens by his comment about the window in St Luke's of the Prophetess Anna.

The reflective poetry of all the contributors to *Faith, Flint & Footstep* is profound, moving and takes us farther in our understanding of who we are, how we live. The last words come from seven-year-old Verity, putting her thoughts in a prayer:

> Dear God, Please let children be free
> So they can be happy
> And play with their friends. – Amen.

Words do sustain us, they can help us to build kindness and empathy; here in St Luke's Church is a place of beginnings, of beauty, a place of the heart.

+Richard Lewes

The Right Reverend Richard Jackson DipHE MSc MA
Bishop of Lewes

The Ascension, east window, St Luke's

Matthew's flowers and light

As we live our truths, we will communicate across all barriers, speaking for the sources of peace. All the poems of our lives are not yet made.

Muriel Rukeyser, *The Life of Poetry*

Detail of the Annunciation, east window, St Luke's Church

FAITH, FLINT & FOOTSTEP – AWAKENING POETRY
Evlynn Sharp

At St Luke's, the threshold of church and community spaces is formed of two large wooden doors, mostly kept open. This openness between the sites of worship and everyday event symbolises the heart of St Luke's – a true container of people's prayers, music, creativity, celebrations and customs.

As poet in residence at St Luke's, I have been working with people inside its flint walls and outside in locations such as care homes, private houses; in Brighton General Hospital and by the Pepper Pot bus stop. With the Revd Julie Newson, we would meet people where they are and share the privilege of hearing each individual convey deeply personal aspects of life, loves, loss.

It can be lonely and isolating to live in a community while the world is changing fast: old identities and ways of being in society fall away, everything shifts shape, our rootedness seems to dissolve under our feet. Yet participants in *Faith, Flint & Footstep* reveal a faith in belonging even in these brisk times.

Whether in a local church, a school, a house, a hospital ward, in a family or with a friend, it still appears our beautifully ordinary relationships bring us comfort, inspiration and companionship. Our links with each other keep us together and help us to feel relevant and more alive. Whatever else changes around us, our creativity helps us make sense of our lives and leaves an imprint for future generations.

In creative workshops with local people to generate poems for this book, I have been learning afresh the value of poetry to extend ourselves towards each other. By writing out of our emotions, thought, silencing, struggles, bereavements, every poet here exerts creative energy to a particular attitude and perspective.

A poem exists everywhere in the sound of nature – the musicality of our lives – past, present, future. With every year that goes by something surfaces to come in to fashion or go out; we may discard people, places, objects, yet we are always in relation to those who have gone and those still to come. A poem is a bridge between times. When we make our poems together, we affirm the freedom of our own voice, our truths, our determination to connect.

By unfolding St Luke's parish story from layers of words, images and heritage materials, I learned how tradition accommodates change. The present church community does not shy away from conflicts, tensions, people's different beliefs. St Luke's is about co-existence, a place to communicate the real in each individual's life, with understanding and compassion. *Faith, Flint & Footstep* documents history and people's poetic expressions that reveal lives and thinking from moment to unlimited moment.

STONE ON STONE
Julie Newson

If you listen closely,
I'll tell you what I know.

I know we're together
As stone is piled on stone;

The stones live and breathe,
No one stands alone,

And the only way I know,
Is you relate to me.

The tower built of stone on stone,
The community of what we know:

As each one leans,
So each one listens.

The tower of strength
Is the community of faith.

Foundation stone, 1882, east wall

TIME'S COURSE
Basil McDonald

Autumn leaves for winter,
Winter leads to spring,
Somewhere in the course of time,
Summer stumbles in.

Time goes by non-stop:
Tick tock, tick tock,
Tick tock.

Time ticks and tocks
And tocks and ticks,
Sometimes plays
Untimely tricks.

But tock or tick or tick or tock,
Time still goes by non-stop.
Tick tock, tick tock,
Tick tock!

St Luke's Church, detail of flint wall

Detail of St John, stained glass, Lady Chapel

Prayer candle, St Luke's

THE WHISPER, THE FREE
Pauline Seager

I have come and it is time you hear me,
Standing in the shadows;

So long a whisper in the room.
Not daring to share or join in,

Waiting for a sign
To wash away clouds of doubt,

Being someone who stood back in wonder
Of your shining light and brightness.

The days of walking behind;
Of travelling but not knowing,

Thoughts and ideas never escaping
But staying locked within the box

Of unknown. I am now here,
Strong and able to offer, to give

And enjoy being part of everything.
Don't be afraid, I will support and care.

But the darkness has gone;
The energy to be heard is spreading out

Like the tide; we will be strong
Together. I will not be afraid.

THE CANDLE BEGINS
Pam Sykes

It is better to speak
Before the moment passes
And the chance is gone.
Before regret sets in.

Be bold; be confident.
Share your dreams, your feelings,
Make that link.

Say what you want to say,
The things hidden deep down,
Locked away in embarrassment
And fear.

Time is not always on our side
So take a deep breath,
And start that journey

Before the candle begins to flicker
And goes out.

East wall, vicarage garden

IN THE BEGINNING
Michael L. Belton

Christ is a friend, peace is spring,
And my wish is to leave
The world in peace for all,
For One church;

And the heart carries
An even deeper prayer –
In the silence,
The peace …

And peace be like spring
Going into summer,
Peace be between nations,
Peace be between countries;

Peace be in the world,
Peace be like spring.

PRECIOUS TO ME, A PRAYER
Peter Burrows

Precious to me is the environment,
It is God's creation,
So precious;

And we should be looking after
The environment, God's creation,
So precious, for the next generation;

Precious to me is God's creation,
Precious to me is the environment,
Precious to me is the next generation.

And today my prayer is for peace,
My prayer is for the needy,
My prayer is for social services.

Today, so precious: the prayer,
The environment,
The next generation;

God's creation,
God's precious creation,
Precious to me.

Fr Michael presides at a Sunday service, St Luke's

POETRY, PRAYER AND SILENCE *Michael Forrest*

The best poetry and prayers find a response in us to life and to death. They mysteriously take over the moment if we engage with their silences and language, becoming our self for now.

The experience of discovering silences within prayers we love and live is like a death within and a re-acquaintance with life. It is humbling and emptying, leading into a new resolve to engage with ourselves and with our neighbour. Prayers make us realise we have to take life from here.

The *Wisdom of Solomon* shows: 'While all things have been in quiet silence, the Almighty Word has leapt down into our life.' We have been graced to live with our neighbour and ourselves, witnessing 'everlasting silence' that St John of the Cross knows 'the soul has to hear'. The Word ushers in a silence that cries out for response.

Prayers and poems are framed by silences, which anyone reading in church has to communicate. The best prayers bring us into a space, a "room" where we belong, and we can live anew in love with our neighbour and ourselves. We are no longer in the prison of our world and thoughts. Whilst aware of the choice of words and meaning, we can transcend situations and respond to the inner self. We are free to praise, and this moment

of richness becomes the 'peace that passes all understanding'.

In prayer and poetry we rediscover our connectedness with God, which is bound up in solidarity with our neighbour. In *New Year Letter*, the poet W H Auden writes: 'O every day in sleep or labour/Our life and death are with our neighbour,/And love illuminates again/The city and the lion's den …'

This reflection of our neighbour's part in our growth echoes back across five centuries from an early monastic teacher, Anthony the Great, who leaves a trail of spiritual footsteps. He observes a greater concern about our neighbour can involve 'a dying to self, that is a death to all things which block and intrude between God and others.' It is our neighbour who helps us hear a death sentence to our living of life only on our own terms.

We can get closer to knowing who our neighbour is, who we are, and when silence breaks the stream of words around us. Our words are life-giving and life-forming, yet they might strengthen self-illusions. If we follow in the footsteps of Moses, there is an invitation to 'fear not, stand still, and see the salvation of the Lord', to hold our peace into another level of language and experience, to let a formative silence happen.

LET HUMANITY RETURN
Janet Freeland

I pray for the oppressed,
For women who have no identity
Who exist in form only.

They have no voice,
They have no power.
They are helpless.

They exist only for others
To control them
In whatever way they wish.

Support them I pray.
Support those who fight on their behalf.

Change the hearts of those responsible
And let humanity return.

MY PRAYER
Jean Grant

I believe my prayer for peace may bear fruit:

Freedom of worship and speech may be
For all beleaguered women;

Evil may cease, of women being bought
And sold into various forms of slavery;

Integrity of service may return
In those in whom trust is placed;

I may live my life as truly
As God may wish it;

I dare to believe I may be
His humble faithful servant

In all my dealings,
Throughout my life.

PRAYER IN ITSELF
(Extract)
Jean Grant

Silence is solace for the soul,
Prayer a plea for patience;

Too many words add to the burden
Of the Cross,

Sharpen the nails,
The lash,

The hurt of derision.

Pulpit Crucifix, St Luke's Church

VOCATION, REFLECTION, DIALOGUES

And where the words of women are crying out to be heard, we must each of us recognise our responsibility to seek those words out, to read them and share them and examine them in their pertinence to our lives.

Audre Lorde, *The Transformation of Silence into Language and Action*

Detail of Prophetess Anna, stained glass, St Luke's Church

Stations of the Cross, St Luke's Church

GROUNDBREAKING FOOTSTEPS: Three ordained women – with links to St Luke's – dialogue on their vocation and realities of frontline ministry.

The Revd Shirley Ford, the Revd Alison Letschka and the Revd Julie Newson shake tradition through following their vocation to reach ordination in the Church of England. By responding to their calling, the women create an imprint of achievement that can encourage others to take risks, make choices and change.

As the present Deacon in Charge of St Luke's, Julie puts her energies into social engagement, strengthening community links and cultivating goodwill. What she does is offer a ministry that is inclusive, reliable and accessible. The welcoming atmosphere of St Luke's reflects her firm commitment to equity.

After attending St Luke's for nearly 25 years and finding her vocation, Alison Letschka is team vicar of St Mary's Church, Bexley. Her ministry seeks to inspire people to cherish the heritage of the medieval Church with its continuum of worship across 800 years, and to find a source of peace pertaining to their lives.

Shirley Ford is one of the earliest ordained women priests of the 1990s, becoming a stipendiary minister in the Guildford Diocese. Retiring to Brighton, she is an active member of St Luke's and a visiting priest who presides and preaches in local Anglican Churches.

In this discussion, the women talk about their experiences, their struggles, strong intent and aspirations over three decades of ministry, which add to the long narrative of the church and increase knowledge.

VOCATION, ORDINATION

ALISON I started coming to St Luke's in 1980. As time went by, Julie and I became aware we were encouraged to have fund-raising collections to help in making more men priests! But in the 80s and 90s came debates about women's ordination. I got to a point when I felt a call, which took a long time to work out. Although I thought I could not face the process, things fell into place.

In the beginning, our vicar could not support me, he was not comfortable with women's ordination. I had to move from St Luke's; it was sad as my husband and I had many friendships here. But later I did a course with Julie, then I trained full time in Cambridge. In 2009, I was ordained as a priest by a retired Bishop.

SHIRLEY Age 50, I felt a nudge from within. After an accident, a long time in hospital gave me time to think. I doubt if there would have been a vocation otherwise. In my days, vicars were men. Yet I had a feeling of wanting to do more and a good relationship with the vicar in my local village who asked why I did not go forward to be a deacon. It all happened in six weeks; I was interviewed in Derby, and I was ordained deacon in 1990, priested in 1994.

Had I been rejected, it would have been different. I was steered through the system by people who were pro-women. But some women were against our ordination! And I remember an incident in a vestry – when I came in, male priests turned to the wall, turning their backs on me and not speaking.

JULIE Vocation does not go away. I first thought about it from age 23 but I was age 43 – ten years ago – when I was ordained. For me, it was about seeing someone else do the job and thinking I could do that. When I first asked questions, I was put down and told to forget it. So ordination looked like it might be possible but I got the message it was not – and I had a whole convoluted journey of 20 years.

I started thinking it was the right end, but it seemed like a dead end. I was even told I might not be bright enough! After the church first said no, my relationship with God was in a mess. I was sure God wanted me to do this work; I was backed by people with deep personal faiths, people whom I trusted. I persisted but it was not plain sailing. Women ordained as deacons used to be seen as a token gesture in the Chichester Diocese.

Detail of the Mother and Child, stained glass, Lady Chapel

Detail of St Luke's winged ox and footstep, external sign board

WOMEN ROLE MODELS AT ST LUKE'S

ALISON We were pushing the boundaries very slightly at St Luke's. In 1987, Julie said we should have something for Women's World Day of Prayer. The big thing was we brought in a woman to preach – Sister Alison Rickard of the Church Army. No woman had ever preached from the pulpit at St Luke's before. Then Julie started her process to be ordained. So St Luke's has been important in the whole process of my ordination, it made a big impact on my life. Yet there were no women role models – we had to find our own. And Julie became a role model, now having her ministry here at St Luke's. We take the faith as seriously as men.

DOUBTS, RULES, DIFFERENCES

SHIRLEY I have no doubts I am doing the right thing. It does not make me immune to people who have different views, I respect those views if thought-through and expressed appropriately. All the rules are man-made. People have walked out on me. It is laughable, but it hurts as well. Younger women do not have the same discrimination we have had.

JULIE Ministries by women brought about an amount of radical change. Discrimination can still be an issue. We are not victims, though.

ALISON Being in charge is different from being a curate. Some men do not know how to be around me. But it is hard when you have been indoctrinated, part of your identity.

Parishioners, especially older people, although they are happy to accept a woman, find it more difficult than they thought.

SHIRLEY Historically, before us there were hundreds of women struggling to get where we are. We paved the way. So people have changed their minds about working with women, and there is humility in the Anglican Church.

JULIE As a woman Deacon in Charge of a parish, the work breaks ground all the time since it is collaborative, unthreatening and involves sharing. I want to keep bringing people together in this way.

MINISTRIES, FUTURE

SHIRLEY I was lucky, I was made to feel I was in the right place, doing the right thing. I always feel a flutter of nerves before doing the sermon, you can influence so many people. Some of my most meaningful work has been at deathbeds and funerals. Praying with people who are close to death and with the bereaved family. Now I am retired, I do not know people in the same way. I still do services including sermons. I want to do as much as possible.

ALISON It is my responsibility to help people through the major events in their lives. I want to keep the profile high, and to make a friendly church where people love each other. There is a different dynamic going on. I want to confront any difficult issues instead of pretending.

SHIRLEY I think the church is going to be different; it has to change. I do not think we can be precious. I feel sometimes priests think whatever they say, God is in their church. It is so much greater than only that. What Julie does is touch people with the church, taking it out there.

ALISON To keep people's interest is part of my work, so they can find this faith community and their vocation to develop – although I do not see many who have that commitment. One of the hardest things about being in charge is you are on your own, which can be very isolating.

JULIE It has to be different. There is this church of flint, stone and cement here for 130 years. I would like to think it is still here in another 130 years. A Victorian building and music can influence and shape the way things are done. I recognise some people may not come for a Sunday service in that traditional, formal setting. You can tweak customs yet only to a certain point, it cannot be changed completely. You have to get the balance right. Collaborative ministry has to be the way if you want to reach out to people. Starting from the right place, where the message is love and light.

Sacred altar stone, high altar, St Luke's

FAITH OVER 80 YEARS
Jean Collins

I never really moved far. My faith is important.
I met friends at school, two girls, June and Joan,
They went to St Luke's Church; I went with them.
When I was 12, I made my first communion,
My friends took communion at the same time;
I had that bright Easter morning – I looked up

At the window over the high altar –
The brightness of the sun came through
And the different colours; Mum came with me.

My brother and my father were carpenters.
I worked at M&S. I got a watch after 25 years.
It's engraved. My years there were quite good.
I would never have worked on a Good Friday
Or an Easter Sunday, either. I left and went back
To St Luke's in 1979. I joined the choir. I recall

Years ago, an organist was not pleased with the way
We had sung; he never played the second verse!
After I joined the choir, I had a fall. I lost confidence.

I wish for good health and help for all people.
So much strife in the world; people hell-bent
On destruction, on death – some are so young.
Up here on Albion Hill, we have students –
Nice, decent youngsters. And badgers –
They are all God's creatures!

My faith has always been very important.
Once, a man talked about male priesthood,
And I asked him, 'Has He not called women!?!'

Every day I go out, I'm helped to come back.
I need the help more than ever now.
I need the church more than ever.

RETROSPECTIVE
Geraldine Pedroza

That was then.
Now is now.
That was seeking.
Now is waiting?
No, not waiting.
More … abiding.

East window, centre panel, St Luke's Church

IN SURVIVAL, TO FIND
(For Audre Lorde)
Evlynn Sharp

Touching down in history
There is the real experience
Of anonymous women
Suffering scold, cut, spikes
Of curtailment – the branks,

A punishment made to lock
Each woman into silences,
Isolating us from her voice,
Leading her from language
Into wordless surrender;

Names move on unknown,
Banished voices weaken.
A woman leans more
Into the corner of listening

Instead of speaking; back
Behind the now old face
Of those not meant to survive,
And any descendants who arrive
In her place must look
Beyond words and fears
To find women wronged

In the mouth, in a heart,
Must search for beginnings
And spread out endings
To re-mark a moment
Where women wept,

The imprints of their lives
Lost in the iron. We must not wait.
Years have already gone,
We need to roar out
Each woman's silent sacrifice,
And remember the hurt,
The harm done,
The long falling
Women survive.

Angel, reredos painting

BE REMEMBERED …
Evlynn Sharp

As a woman snapping out
Of a rolling placeless map,
And landing in those shoes
To be worn day in, day out,
Not too far through the heel,
Re-softening a myth;
Sparks on stone and plant,
The unused path.

Two Angels, reredos paintings

Shadow on tiled floor, chancel

DIRECTIONS
Angela Goodman

The North Star
In my celestial map
Makes me feel very small
As I look up into the night sky.

Sometimes the Moon is there,
If there is no cloud;
It's always different,
A different picture, shape, colour.

There might be a planet or two,
Venus or Mars,
I wish I had more than a glimpse
Because they are soon gone;

The sky makes me feel sad, too,
Because my feet rest so firmly
On the ground;
No shortcuts here on earth
But plenty of obstacles,

Other people's rules,
Expectations, demands;

How can I navigate round
This man-made map?

MAP OF MY LIFE
Janet Hardacre

The map of my life is like
Road signs at a crossroads
In a country lane,

Every day people rush by in cars,
Or may even walk by
As a party of ramblers,
But most people never stop.

The signs are there
To point to what's beyond
Or on the other side;

The signs are there in all weathers –
All seasons – and may be obliterated
By snow, but underneath
The sign is still there.

The names of places on the signs
Can be funny or not pronounced
The way they are spelt –
But all can be found
On a local map of Ordinance Survey;

One day, there may be tourists,
Or inquisitors – people who say,
'I wonder where that leads to …'

And follow the directions
To discover a lovely village,
Or hamlet, or a church,
Or area of natural beauty

And then tell everyone –
Or just their friends –
This discovery.

Russell Robinson (centre), the Revd Julie Newson and Trevor Jordan-Jones administer Holy Communion

Inside St Luke's, wooden pews and cross-stitch kneelers

DIFFERENT BOUNDARIES, DIFFERENT UNDERSTANDING

Now in his 40s, *RUSSELL ROBINSON* has been part of St Luke's Church for 30 years. Over time, he has been forced to confront his conditioning and question his responses to issues such as the ordination of women. Russell – a trustee of the parochial church council – looks at the nature of change, and his own deepening sense of vocation through his experiences of life at St Luke's.

RUSSELL No matter where I am in the world, I'm thinking of St Luke's on a Sunday, something is missing in the pattern of the week if I don't go. St Luke's is my extended family so sometimes we disagree, even occasionally offend people, but in the end find ways to work through disagreements.

My earliest connection with St Luke's was being allowed to come to the Youth Club. I was 10 years old. My parents had a faith but they never felt worthy enough for church, maybe because of their working-class background. Things could be difficult at home for me, and St Luke's was a place of stability and security.

One of the key strengths of St Luke's is its liturgical development, which reflects the truths we believe. Worship is important, care and attention go into it. Music is also important, a powerful and massive gift in the Anglican Church, which helps us to focus on the Sacrament, to focus our prayer.

St Luke's has gone through some lows. At times the welcome, energy and preaching began to break down. But in the last few years St Luke's has been growing and thriving, the quality of teaching and preaching is high and accessible.

I continue to have reservations about the ordination of women to the priesthood. Faith can be tested across difficult boundaries, people's vulnerabilities and the idea of Christian ministry. While the community at St Luke's has come to a different mind on the issue of women's ordination, my family and I feel a valued part of the church family.

Since Deacon Julie has been in charge, we have a clearer vision and our facilities are widely used. The reality is having a Deacon in Charge brings a variety of approaches and perspectives and a leadership built on service.

St Luke's is so much more than a building. The most memorable day of my life was the day my wife Emma and I were married here. In the months before, we felt supported by love and prayers. After the wedding, friends remarked on how the Nuptial Mass was a transforming element of their faith journey; it was celebrated in such a loving and inclusive community. My prayer for the future at St Luke's is we continue to find new and imaginative ways to serve the local community, for people to feel loved and accepted.

FORGIVENESS, LOCAL – GLOBAL

We cannot afford to forget any experience, not
even the most painful.

Dag Hammarskjöld

Detail of Saint Peter, stained glass, St Luke's Church

Angels, Lady Chapel

FORGIVENESS: INNER AND OUTER CALLING

MARINA CANTACUZINO is Founder of The Forgiveness Project. In this feature she writes about why individuals choose forgiveness in times of hurt and trauma and considers the wider circumstance of collective grief.

For some people forgiveness is a personal decision and part of their own self-healing process, which liberates them from the resentment and anger holding them back. Others feel inspired to forgive, because they experience compassion for those who have hurt them. And many see a spiritual value in forgiveness, because they recognise we are all connected and in some way responsible for the pain in the world.

According to Stephen Levine in *Unattended Sorrow*, if deep wounds remain within us then 'the inner war continues.' It is easy to see the value of forgiveness when dealing with personal hurts and inner grievances, but when it comes to rebuilding communities post conflict, forgiveness can be useful by aiding post-traumatic reconciliation and building a sustainable peace.

By creating a foundation for dialogue, inducing a shift in mind-sets and transforming harmful attitudes, forgiveness can build bridges between opposing parties and facilitate the re-humanisation of the "other".

'It is the responsibility of the living to heal the dead,' says Alexandra Asseily, creator of the Garden of Forgiveness in Lebanon. She has written extensively about the repetitive nature of conflict; how consciously (and unconsciously) held grievances are received by each new generation through an ancestral bond that can only be released through forgiveness and compassion.

Recognising the humanity of the "other" means recognising we are all capable of harm, given the right circumstances. The Russian author and dissident Aleksandr Solzhenitsyn spoke of this in *The Gulag Archipelago*: 'If only there were evil people somewhere insidiously committing evil deeds, and it were necessary only to separate them from the rest of us and destroy them. But the line dividing good and evil cuts through the heart of every human being. And who is willing to destroy a piece of his own heart?'

Forgiveness and reconciliation is about shifting and transforming people's attitudes, prejudices. Forgiveness is not an act of kindness from the victim's generosity, but a re-humanising gift emphasising the humanity of the perpetrator. In the softening of positions comes the acknowledgement and possibility of each side's complicity.

Take the story of Ghazi Briegeith, a Palestinian whose brother was killed at a checkpoint in 2000. He is a member of the grassroots organisation of bereaved Palestinians and Israelis, Parents Circle. He says: 'I saw the soldier as a victim of the occupation just as my brother was, just as I am still. … I can't force my brother's kids to forgive. But I can show them that far more valuable than a violent response is opening your heart to reconciliation and peace. I can show them that opening a new page is their only hope of living a better life than ours.'

For information about the work of The Forgiveness Project, visit the website: www.theforgivenessproject.com

Detail of casting lots, stained glass, east window, St Luke's

Detail of the Crucifixion, stained glass, sun and moon, St Luke's

QUESTIONS
Rebecca Whitley-Jones

How did I become this – me?
Like a car starting out on a journey;
Is this my destination?

Or am I to travel deeper,
Through the winding roads of life?

For I never was set on this –
Like stepping stones across a stream,
I took each one step at a time.

But why do people feel the need to judge?
Is it insecurities within themselves?

Or just curiosity?
Perhaps admiration?
This is part of being human –

THIS is what makes us human.
If we did not judge,

Would it make us better as individuals?
Perhaps not; perhaps we would find
Other faults add to our insecurities.

TIMES TO FORGIVE
Janet Freeland

Forgiveness is difficult to grasp
When you are hurting,
Yet I know that unless you can forgive,
The hurt remains and often grows.
I'm not a forgiving person,
I know that,
So it is difficult,
I can't rise above the hurt felt,
And I stay silent.
There have been times in the past
When I would have liked to forgive,
It would have eased the pain,
When personal feelings are involved
And words used to inflict pain.
Or there are other times
When simply interference by another
In something you perceive as yours alone
Is viewed with bad feelings.
I would like to forgive relatives,
Family members, because of what I know
They have done; but I can't,
I see it as a betrayal
Of what I believe.

FORGIVENESS
Angela Goodman

How can I forgive?
It would mean diving down
Into the depths of my soul;

I'm so scared of what I might find,
It's too difficult,
Supposing I lose that part of myself
That keeps me alive?

It's much easier
To hold on to my suffering,
So painful but familiar,
Reassuring.

Where do I go from here?
I can't see a signpost
Or a direction indicator,

So I slip back into something
Like the routine I had before,
Yet something is nagging me
To reject and rediscover
What lies underneath;

It could be a nightmare
Or the Promised Land;
Is my faith strong enough
To sustain me on the journey?

Doubt is my constant companion,
She doesn't want to be left at home.

St Michael, above west door

TOWARD FORGIVING HANDS
(**Extract**)
Wendy Horsfield

Hands at times are quite often not logical.
Hands are like a vessel to do many things,
Some good and some not so good ...
The act of writing using hands can offend,
Hurt and lie. People may believe lies, use
The lies written down, justify atrocities.

The hand writes down rules and laws
To follow; statutory laws are laid visible
By printing them down into pages,
Workers in factories put these pages
Together, to make manifestos
That place people against each other.

These manifestos and laws written down
Can make a simple life into a life of chaos.
But also hands can write a defence,
Take up a cause, protect,
And find the truth, the forgiveness,
Set some people free.

CREATE, COMMUNITY, RELEASE

Let yourself be silently drawn by the stronger
pull of what you really love.

Rumi

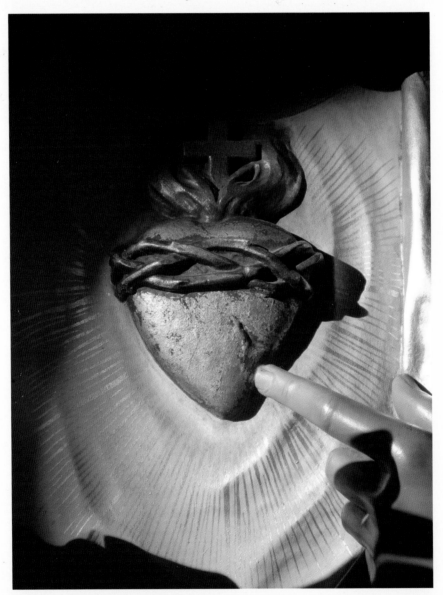

Detail of the Sacred Heart of Jesus, St Luke's Church

FAITH, FLINT & FOOTSTEP: OUR PARABOLIC LIVES

The Reverend Julie Newson

I have come to think about *Faith, Flint & Footstep* as a parable itself; our lives are open to stories and interpretations. At St Luke's and throughout its parish, people have been giving their poetic stories as the resource for this book.

Putting together the book with Evlynn Sharp, the church's poet in residence, we would give thanks for people sharing their recollections and the historical materials that signify how our lives are shaped by social conditions, culture and creativity, instincts and meanings.

Among the themes of *Faith, Flint & Footstep*, which would sometimes catch a home in my Sunday sermons, I find steps of faith and the church's foundation stone inform my thinking symbolically about heritage. And the flint of St Luke's makes me realise the building holds unexpected things together, even as the growing ground of a rare plant on the outside that is almost invisible.

As a focus of contemplation, this flinty wall resonates with the scripture passage of hiding in the cleft of a rock: the absolute trust all can embrace our source and press on farther than understanding.

As I wonder about creativity and share with others in writing reflective poems and prayers, I know the beginning in us is the Word so there the essence of the eternal within. We contain a fertile imagination, and the reality that our lives are full of parables. In fact, life itself is parabolic. We live by building up our insights.

I believe Jesus, the master teacher, knew this truth. He uses parables to illustrate a teaching, to share the divine Word. We can find inspiration here to search for our own parables that point to a way of being in the world and wider meaning.

There are times in life that necessitate parabolic speech. There may be no other way to experience a situation that is painful, denied, confusing. The force of a parable that is spoken aloud can break resistances to find what is necessary to hear personally and among others for our own particular concerns.

Yet telling a parable will not secure answers, and sometimes we tame parables with attempts at allegory. We hope for our works to be acts in which characters and events are understood as representing our faith and expressing a moral meaning.

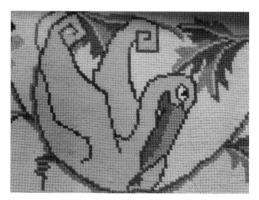 

Pelican and winged ox from cross-stitch altar rail kneeler, designed by Patrick Letschka, St Luke's Church

Detail of the Ascension footprints, east window, St Luke's Church

PATIENCE

But we need patience to let parables work as figurative expressions of mystery, from the imprint of our master teacher.

At its etymological core, a parable is not a straightforward, interpretative exercise. It is something thrown alongside, "para" meaning alongside and "bole" from the root to "throw" or "cast". Parallel lines never meet.

Likewise the parable that is put alongside may never meet the subject of its message. There is an alignment that forces a meandering back and forth between two interpretations, fluidity and change, open to each individual depending on influences at any time and place.

We interpret a parable differently, and as the parallel lines will never meet along a parallel journey, there is no end to what is possible for us to encounter. Jesus tells parables, his entry into the world – as the kingdom of God – is meant to be unsettling. To walk alongside Christ's presence in our parabolic lives means sometimes we will catch glimpses of the kingdom and its meaning.

Whatever example is cast alongside parables of life, it is never the means to be fully understood, although our minds make that our starting point.

The most exciting fact about messages delivered to the first disciples in parables is that more than two thousand years later we can absorb new interpretations that make sense to us and are unfixed.

St Andrew, stained glass

EXPLORATION

Our master teacher tells parables not for explanation but for exploration, not to present answers but to engage the imagination. Parables are not for certainties about faith but for discoveries about how faith works.

Jesus invites us to both talk in and listen to parables as something happens in the unfathomable encounter.

Working on a parable is a different experience from reflecting on the purpose of one we hear. A parable can be a useful guide, and everyone could find one to write. The parable I would tell in Queen's Park centres on *Faith, Flint & Footstep*. There is no point in pushing too hard.

When I asked my church warden to make visible the foundation stone outside of St Luke's, which could not be seen, he worked faithfully to pull back the veil of weeds, bushes – bringing in new light.

The stone of our creative faith has stories to tell of people who are placing their steps alongside.

Detail of disciple witnessing the Ascension, east window, St Luke's

WRITERS OF THE SUNDAY SCHOOL: *thoughts on footsteps, community*

THE FOOTSTEP
Alan

Long journeys are made
From little footsteps.
Footsteps take you and me
Everywhere.
No footstep and no snowflake
Is ever the same as another.

HAPPY
Tanwen

When I'm happy my footsteps gallop.

FAVOURITE
John

My favourite footstep
Is a golden footstep in the sand …

BETTER WORLD
Billy

The world will be better
With a smile, recycle, a heart.

TO HELP THE WORLD!
Elliott

Smile! My feet take me on the football field.

IMPRINTS
Millie

My footprints go in a book.
Millie footprints go in Sunday School.

Image by Ruth of the Sunday School; detail of
Jesus' feet, Sacred Heart statue

PURPOSES
Ruth

My footsteps sound like drums.
My footsteps are purpose.
My footsteps are loud.
My footsteps are funny shapes.

A BETTER PLACE
Ashli and Acer

Things to make the world
A better place: stop pollution!
Give homeless a home.

THIS IS OUR PRAYER TO GOD
Zane

We pray for the feet travelling
Across the ocean
To live a happy, safe life.
Crash, bash, splish, splash,
Sailing through the rough
And calm. The sea is glorious.
I feel the water tingling, soon
My feet will be in the sand.
This is what I pray. – Amen.

THE FOOTSTEPS
Kayley

Footstep, footstep, on the ground.
Soundly. Trying. Secretly.

PRECIOUS TO ME (GROUP POEM)
Naomi, Emily, Marah, Tanwen

Precious are heart jewels.
Precious to me are my teeth.
Precious is my old news book.
Precious is a purple pebble.
Precious to me is a necklace.
Precious to me are flowers.

TO MAKE A BETTER WORLD
Katie

Get people to grow flowers
In their garden.
Help nearly extinct animals …
Make more homeless shelters.

UNTITLED
Carmen

Silent – breaker. Bright – destroyer.
Foot – warmer. Ground – placer.
Outside – wearer. Nothing better.
Footsteps.

FOR CHILDREN OF THE WORLD, REFUGEES
Olivia

My prayer is no more children will die,
They will have warm and happy homes,
Nice friends, and live good lives
With enough food to eat.
And dear God,
Bless everyone who died
And help those who are dying.
Make sure you are always with them
Even in hard times. – Amen.

GIFT FOR THE WORLD
Verity

I would like to give to the world
Money and food;
I would like to give to the world
Water and love;
I would give to the world doctors.
I would give to the world shelter.

MY OFFERING TO YOU
Evie

I would give to the world:
Everyone – food and water;
Everyone – a shelter.

I would give to the world:
Healthy environment;
Free health service.

I would give to the world:
Love and family.

FOOTSTEPS
Dylan

Feet playing football
On the bright, green grass.
On the dusty road
Trudging past.
Sidling slowly
Through the trees.·
Excited children
Paddling in the
Sea.

Children in the Easter garden, St Luke's

Bouncy castle, St Luke's fair

From altar towards community space,
St Luke's Church

Hymn number board on stone pillar

HOME
Pauline Seager

The door beckons – this familiar door,
Brass handles and glass to see inside;
A glimpse of what awaits, the embrace
It will give me – my home.
The day has been long and difficult,
I yearn for the known, for comfort.
I go through the door, and there
It awaits me – my home.

Someone is playing music. Something
I know, it touches my memory with joy.
I hum along, my face breaks into a smile.
My home. I recognise without thinking.
Old furniture stands firm. And homely smells;
The scent of flowers, cooking, and polish, smoke
Mingled into one. The building surrounds me
Like a blanket making all things better.

My home. Late summer, the sun is low in the sky
Now. The light shines through large windows,
Spreads its rays as a carpet before me,
Draws me in and sets me down;
Colours bounce off walls and highlight beauty
Within. My home. A place of peace, concern, love,
Friendship, kindness, challenge; always changing,
Always supporting, always there. My home,

I have known for a lifetime, part of my being,
A place where my family has grown
And with the grace of God will continue to grow.
The place from where I will make my final journey.
A place where I have had many celebrations, joys,
Also much sadness. My home. A place of laughter,
Conversation, conflict and resolution,
Alongside excitement and spirit.

A place for everyone; the door is open,
Love is here. My home can be shared
By all. I will go out and tell everyone
About my home: St Luke's Church.

LIVING MY EPISTLE
Julie Newson

I live out my epistle
On the map of the parish;

Many words in my letter,
Many letters on my map;

The map shows the boundaries
And how they change with time.

The epistle of life also changes with time
With nothing as clear as a parish boundary;

I write words to the people
And respond to words from them –

Each writing their own epistle
Among blades of grass on the map;

I have lived out the letter on other maps,
With always flexible boundaries.

And what would be my sign and symbol
On the map? Something bold

And central at the heart of the map
Or small, insignificant in the margins;

Deacons are signposts, bridges
And doorkeepers,

So a sense of direction
Rather than a place might be best?

Detail of tapestry, St Luke and winged ox,
nineteenth-century banner

EACH THE EPISTLE
(Inspired by 2 Corinthians 3)
Evlynn Sharp

A living letter is one woman's life. An age,
A mirror, a teller certain of times past
Beginning pertinent words to this letter,
Moving through constancies and graves.

Upon the living epistle of myself,
I want to accept every experience,
Every rite of solitude and root
Where shoots of life stem, surprise,

Yet never demise – this living letter
Is the action of love as written now –
Stretching the future, common ground.

DOWN THE ROAD
Chris Whitley-Jones

I remember when my Dad and I walked
Onto the South Downs at 4 o'clock
On a humid, summer morning;
Down the garden, past the rhubarb,
Through the gate, across the field,
And up the farm track.

Once on the top of the Downs,
We watch the sunrise,
And then what is there to see?
Rabbits, foxes, and skylarks up above.
Horses in the field,
Lambs and sheep in the barn.

Down onto the road
Past the rifle range, then up the hill
Where we can see Brighton
And the sea in the distance.
What will this place be like
In 20 years' time? Covered in houses?

Or protected
For a future generation
To walk free?

RECOLLECTIONS
Angela Goodman

Childhood outings to Bluebell Woods,
A carpet of lilac as far as I could see.
Ditchling Common
Where I wandered off;
Nan was worried, calling out.

I panicked,
I ran back
Crashing through the thorn bush,
Scratching my arms and legs.
Mum took me and my sister
On picnics to the park,

They stopped, but when I don't know.
I don't recall being happy
Or particularly sad,
I was just there, where I was.
No thought
Of past, present, future;
None of it in my control.

A child gazes at the Cross on the font, St Luke's

THANK YOU TO AN ANGEL
Wendy Horsfield

Thank you for being so kind,
Making me that cup of tea,
At ten past twelve – that act.

Boiling the kettle. In the past,
The kettle and the cup of tea
Would be followed

By reflection. Not being able
To move forward, a fear
I was not worth much.

The ten past twelve cup
Opened up my life –
An angel came down

And created this act.
I am sure of it.
Sixteen years later,

Much learnt,
Much happiness,
I have opened up,

Learned to be me,
To be me with you,
Learned I was sacred.

An act of kindness can change
In one millisecond of time
To a new, wonderful life.

LETTER TO THE FRIEND
Janet Hardacre

I thought of you and wanted to write.
They say all the world is a stage.
What if all the world is a book,
And all the people are chapters?

One chapter to have lessons on love,
And how it is to be shown.
Another on generosity,
And how that is to be won.
Another on hope and compassion,
Are they enough to write about?
Writing to you, I am full of love
For you and humankind.

Writing to you I can be generous
With my time, thoughts, feelings.
I can see a chain letter in the book.
This is the chain letter – pass it on.

Detail of Angel, stained glass, east window, St Luke's Church

REFLECTIONS OF AN ELDER, ST LUKE'S
Elizabeth Wicks

When you are old, you remember old days.
I was born in 1930. A different world.
We had no phones. We had no television.
Never had toys, except for at Christmas.
Never had Easter Eggs, not when I was a child.
We did not feel we had missed out.

We did not consider ourselves poor. But we had food.
Nowadays. Children are hungry in this country.
Nowadays. The values are different.
Nowadays. I pray every night.
What I pray for every night is a peaceful world,
An end to the violence; you can break your heart.

Every night, I pray for peace.
I still pray for those hostages,
Those young Nigerian girls, out of the school,
I pray for the girls, all dropped out of the news,
Who knows what happens to them;
I pray for their families. A different world.

Nowadays, I do not watch much TV.
I have puzzle books. I remember old days:
People could not get behind with their rent;
We used to go over Wild Park at Moulsecoomb;
We always took a walk on Sunday along seafronts.
Family and the church still matter to me.

And nowadays, I have good neighbours.
I like to read in the evening.
I have made my funeral arrangements,
I have chosen my hymns. And I pray,
I would like to see more peace
In the world. A different world.

I LOOK TO SEE WHAT I HAVE
Jean Grant

What do I see, emptiness or fullness?
My own inadequacies,
Or completeness?

What do I see,
In faces of those about me –
Interest or indifference?

I see:
The joy love shows in so many ways.
Old eyes that gleam with wisdom

And compassion. My blessedness
In the gifts bestowed. Tolerance
In the face of prejudice;

God in my inner self,
Support in weakness,
Peace in mind's turmoil.

Queen's Park, south from St Luke's

Prophetess Anna, stained glass, St Luke's Church

According to Fr Steven Foster, it is quite unusual to see the Prophetess Anna represented as an older woman in the stained-glass window of a church. This portrayal connects to Fr Steven's belief in cherishing older people of the church, and in recognition of their wisdom. He remarks: 'The image depicts the Prophetess in her 80s; a woman of prayer who has a significant role, so illuminating of a key moment. In the image is the personal experience for us.'

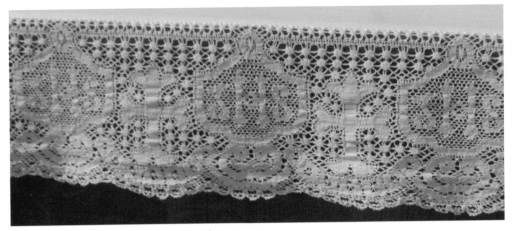

Lace trim, memorial altar, St Luke's Church

LIFE IS FULL
Yvonne Whitley-Jones

I said to my soul, don't analyse the past.
The things I didn't do,
The things I did do and regretted.

The things I did not say,
The things I should've said.

His Spirit is still there,
And he's looking down on me.

Life is full of regrets. The "what-ifs"?
Hindsight is a wonderful thing – or is it?
Yet comforting in a way,

Although he's not here in body,
I know he's watching over me.

Life is full of light-bulb moments.
Things fall into place
Like the pieces of a jigsaw;

It's as though my life had a plan
From the moment I was born,
All mapped out and waiting for me;

We all have to die at some point,
It's a natural thing, a process.

I said to my soul, don't analyse the past;
Concentrate and look to the future.

RECENT LOSS
(For Frank)
Sylvia Reed

I recently lost my husband, I knew
He would not come out of hospital.
I don't know why I thought that,
I did not know what to expect each day.

I feel as if I am in a bubble at present,
And maybe it is going to burst.
I do manage day-to-day, keeping busy –
What if I stop? Will I be a total wreck?

Everybody has been kind to me,
Each day is okay; but night time …
After 5pm, I feel totally alone,
The house is so quiet,
I watch the soaps on TV;

I go out to choir twice a week;
Other nights –
My family and friends do ring me
To make sure I am all right;
I always say I am,

And don't give it much thought
As to how I am feeling.
What can I say now I am alone?
I would just like courage to say
What I am really thinking.

REMEMBRANCE
Rebecca Whitley-Jones

I remember looking, looking
At the small clock face gripping to my wrist,
Almost clinging on for dear life.

10 past 3 didn't seem like a significant time,
Although it was 400-odd miles away;
Seconds just ticking by,

Yet I was blissfully unaware
That those were the last for some
But the longest for others.

10 past 3 is only a time,
But it was the last time,
The last breath,

The last look,
The last touch.

HALF-OPEN DOORS
(For Mary née Moller)
Evlynn Sharp

Today, we gather near the ancestors' home
In Leitir Móir. Waves are pulling in your name,
We're witnessing the pound of memories,

Your ashes from son's hand to soil, Mary,
We're listening as the tribute words to you
Pass round and envelop all in soft lament.

We stand in ground as nourishing still
As when you and I first regard here –
I make a black-and-white photograph,

You are gazing beyond window, frame,
And walls, the peeling scripts
Of your grandparents' house,
Their kin parents before these –

Looking back, I remember
We always talked about rain
Following us from place to place;
We would laugh. Now a mood is turning,

We are returning you home in our heart,
My friend, by the half-open door
Of Leitir Móir,

The Connemara
Of your root,
Of your secret race,
Beneath the Irish oak.

Side doors, St Luke's

Windows, restored in memory of loved ones, Lady Chapel, St Luke's

SOMEONE WHO ...
Pam Sykes

I want to be remembered
As someone who laughed,

Who tried to be kind
Even in the difficult days.

I cannot leave a legacy
To humankind

Like a towering cathedral
With intricate stonework,

A scientific discovery
That changes the world,

A painting of outstanding quality
And beauty,

A memorable, award-winning book,
But I can hope people may smile

When they remember me.
And they were glad in a way

I was a friend,
I shared my joy

With them, I helped to make
The day worthwhile.

CREATION
Steph Busen-Smith

I want to be remembered
For the things I have been part of
And done, created.

I will be remembered differently
By those I knew.
It is not a fixed identity,

Each person will have
Their own memories of me
As I have of them.

Memories are created
And in a kind of flux;
I want to be remembered

By those I love,
My children,
To be remembered ...

For things I have created,
For things I have achieved,
Remembered by who I am.

MUSIC, TRADITION, GRACE

Truly great music brings to expression the states of the soul. This huge nobility enhances the heart and opens the imagination to the deeper mystery and riches of being here.

John O'Donohue, *Divine Beauty*

Detail of nineteenth-century Bevington organ, St Luke's Church

SACRED MUSIC, MOMENTS OF GRACE

The essence of worship in St Luke's Church is tradition-filled music that brings people a sense of unity and atmosphere to anchor and develop their faith. Director of Music *CHRIS WHITLEY-JONES* reflects how church music and the choir's 30-plus voices create a fluid link from present to past when nineteenth-century music would first draw people together in devotion.

From the St Luke's archive, music books dating back over 100 years are evidence of potent organ music and a thriving choir. The Victorian building is typical of what composers of the day such as Stainer and Maunder would have been working with, and Chris feels their sorts of sounds make the music feel authentic and powerful even now.

Chris is deeply committed to the tradition of "high church" liturgy, which gives an excellent stage for the music to serve well within the worship at St Luke's. The choir has a vast and expanding repertoire to choose from that is illustrative of the liturgical seasons. Chris carefully selects music to chime well each year from Advent to Easter and everything in between.

Organist Michael Millyard at music practice, St Luke's

Chris Whitley-Jones, Director of Music

Choir music from the archives, St Luke's Church

WORSHIP

The work of presenting beautiful choral music takes concentration, frequent practice, sincerity and dedication to high standards. Chris' own way of worship is practical, dynamic and done on a weekly basis with the choir.

Through this close work, everyone strives towards perfecting the music to enrich people's lives on Sundays and at other times such as Evensong.

Across three decades as organist and choirmaster at St Luke's, Chris' natural enthusiasm for traditional choral music encourages others to become involved. The choir, which includes his wife and daughter, proceeds to strengthen and grow.

Years ago at church Chris spotted Michael Millyard, his childhood teacher, who also provides knowledge and skills as an organist to support the choir.

Chris continues to develop his abilities and to research musical works, and he is passionate about church music. He studied the organ at school and joined a choir where he became familiar with the liturgy. At university, a request from the chaplain led him to become a church organist.

His roots are firmly planted in the church, and he finds inspiration in composers of organ music such as Olivier Messiaen who in seeing colours when hearing musical chords began to make demanding, complex and absorbing works. Chris accommodates such works – pushing at the boundaries of his musical skills and presenting new challenges to people's lives.

Under Chris' direction, the choir of St Luke's presents music that people can feel is special, when past and present reverberate afresh to communicate truth. The music is accessible to churchgoers and people in the local community for the chance to experience sound and rhythms that touch and connect them.

St Luke's choir offers expertise that stems from singing week by week and engagements at settings such as Portsmouth, Chichester, Winchester, Wells and Bristol Cathedrals plus on CDs of Advent, Lent and Easter music, which builds on work across generations to help others find beauty and harmony within.

SOUNDS TO MY SOUL
Julie Newson

I am saying to my soul
Where is this in between?
Between what I was
And what I shall be,

That means I must be
Where I am?
So what of the past,
And all I remember?

How much forms what
And where I am?
Both the good and the bad,
The easy path,

The challenging mountains,
And everything in between –
Yes, everything in between.
I recall the sounds of some

Who shaped my being,
Others slip into obscurity
With the passing of time,
The current challenges now.

Who knows what is to come?
Who knows the influences
That will unlock new ideas,
Sounds to my soul,

For every note –
Every action –
Is prayer in the making,
Formation of being,

And always,
In between.

The Revd Julie Newson and choir members,
St Luke's

Jane, choir member, receives a birthday candle

PRECIOUS TO ME
Katy Rodda

My boys who sing and dance and play
My friends at church who sing and talk
Friends and others across this beautiful city
Wheels to explore, legs to push hard
Head to learn, thank and think

Detail of nineteenth-century organ, St Luke's Church

EVERYTHING A SEASON
Evlynn Sharp

A time when the voice is pouring
Alto into its counterpart,
A time the incense is climbing
And music is opening us;

A time of flamboyances
Outside flint walls,
A time of unsung intervals
Between two prayers,

A time for releasing scales
Onto the music of a tree;
A time for the loving of life
Being whispered by branches;

A time for silences and song
To form behind a curve, a time
Numbers are rounding up,
Plying for a time to be.

PAST AND FUTURE
Steph Busen-Smith

Now is the time,
Not the past
Or future.

To dwell in the present
Is to see what it brings us.
So much richness is around us.

The past is gone, and the future
Is there to be created.
Memories, though, have their richness

And teach us. Traditions, my faith,
Going to St Luke's
And the services;

Music brings the past
Into what is now,
Brings home continuity.

But now is the time to start
Something new each day, always
A surprise, a new creation.

Detail of *How Beautiful are the Feet* used by church musicians, St Luke's

THE TIMES
Pauline Seager

Now is the time to "sing",
Age brings confidence,
Time brings memories,
People bring relationships,

Knowing when to comfort,
When to laugh,
When to stand firm,
Watching and learning,

Not jumping in and upsetting;
Standing back and looking,
Enjoying silence and colour,
Seeing God's creation

And praising, taking time,
Not running so fast we cannot see.
Having space to do things that please,
Giving more and sharing,

Watching and caring,
Reading books and creating,
Growing plants and painting,
Watching films and singing,

Gone are the days of feeling unsure,
It doesn't matter any more
If things go wrong,
It's not the end,

We can rebuild
And start again.

RETROSPECTION
Evlynn Sharp

Seed by seed begins the spectacle,
Every rhythm, behaviour, pulse,
Life pushes through a parting grain,
Longing is growing its song again;

The uplift and drifting of stardust,
The rare cadence of ancient ones,
The slow in-singing of a language,
Halftones are quivering underfoot.

For where your treasure is,
There will your heart be also.

St Luke 12:34

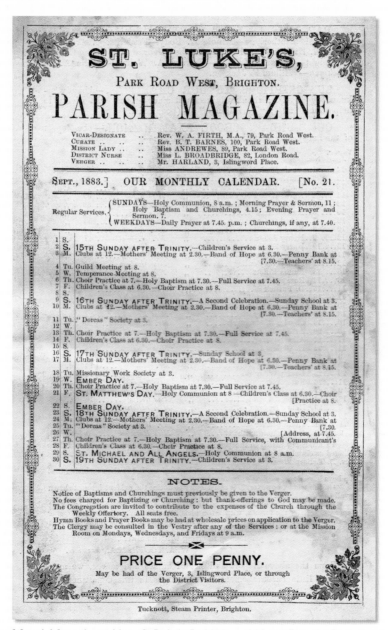

Material from the archives, St Luke's. In 2015, parishioner Dorothy Barnett
recalls this 1883 magazine was printed a year before her father was born.

Brighton Daily Gazette & Sussex Telegraph extract of news report, April 17, 1885, 'Opening Ceremony Yesterday' of St Luke's Church

Trowel used for laying the foundation stone, St Luke's Church, 1882

1. *Brighton Daily Gazette & Sussex Telegraph*, Friday, April 17, 1885 (with kind permission of *The Argus*)

2. The Revd Dr I R Phelps, *St Luke's Church, Queen's Park, Brighton: A Souvenir History and Guide to the Church & Parish (1974)*

THE HISTORY AND HERITAGE OF ST LUKE'S CHURCH AND ITS PARISH
Louise Peskett

The creation of the parish; building of the church

St Luke's Church was consecrated on 16 April 1885, which the *Brighton Daily Gazette & Sussex Telegraph* described in an article the next day: 'The service was rendered in a manner at once solemn and beautiful, and the Bishop delivered a most appropriate sermon …'[1] The ceremony was followed by a tea party for 300 parishioners. The article describes the church as 'a very substantial building of handsome Gothic architecture, the roof covered with Burgess Hill tiles, the nave and aisles of pith pine, the pulpit and font of Caen stone.'

The first vicar was the Revd Walter Firth who made the church the heart of the community, working to establish educational and charitable activities in the densely populated and poor parish.

The foundation stone of the new church was laid earlier on 18 October 1882 – St Luke's Day – by the Bishop of Chichester, the Rt Revd Richard Durnford, and the trowel he used for the purpose is still kept in the church. The architect was Sir Arthur Blomfield (1829-1899) who designed St Luke's with an emphasis on simplicity. It is built of flint with mouldings and stone window dressings.

Blomfield was the architect who went on to rebuild the Chapel Royal in North Street and, with his sons, St John the Evangelist Church near Preston Park, as well as the Royal College of Music and the Bank of England in London. Historic England awarded St Luke's Church with Grade II listed status in 1999.

By 1885 the church was completed except for a proposed 160-foot spire that was, as it turned out, too costly to build. The Revd I R Phelps, vicar of St Luke's from 1968-76, writing a church history in 1974, suggests the missing spire is not to be lamented: 'Fortunately for future generations this was never built.'[2]

The new church did have earlier beginnings – in 1875, a 'chapel of ease' had been built across the road as a place where local people could worship. It was constructed on the west side of Queen's Park Road opposite the present St Luke's but became too small to accommodate a growing parish. The chapel of ease was destroyed by fire in the 1970s. The building was demolished; a sheltered housing scheme of flats – Sidney Tidy House – now stands there.

Postcard from 1905 depicting St Luke's Church, Queen's Park Road, Brighton *(James Gray Collection, the photographic archive of The Regency Society; with kind permission)*

The chapel of ease and the anonymous benefactress

The chapel of ease was referred to as St Luke's Mission Church and St Luke's School Church since it served as church, school and parish hall. The area was expanding and largely working class. Many of the streets that form today's Queen's Park and Hanover areas came into being in the 1860s and 1870s. The chapel of ease had a surrounding population of over 3,000 people; it was so fully attended the decision was made in 1880 to found the parish of St Luke as well as building the new, bigger church.

Preparatory work on the new church started in 1881 on a site opposite that was purchased for £900 next to the then Queen's Park Cricket Club. The cost was borne by a donor who wanted to be known, according to the *Brighton Daily Gazette & Sussex Telegraph*, as 'an anonymous benefactress'.[1] She was, in fact, a Miss E F I Elliott, the youngest daughter of the Revd Henry Venn Elliott and niece of Charlotte Elliott, writer of over 150 hymns.

There are hints the church's birth was not straightforward with reports it was built 'after surmounting very considerable and … unprecedented difficulties.'[2] The details remain 'unknown'.[3]

In 1886, the vicarage, on Queen's Park Terrace, was built with the help of 'anonymous' Miss Elliott, at a cost of £2,200. In 1887, a large parish hall was built on Elm Grove for the use of the north end of the parish. This hall was sold and is now the Brighton Trades Labour Club and Institute Ltd, Elm Grove. In 1968, St Matthew's Church closed and its congregation transferred to St Luke's. In 1974, the parish of St Luke merged with other parishes – St Martin's, St Alban's, St Wilfrid's, St Saviour's – into a single team ministry, the parish of the Resurrection. After 35 years, the team ministry and parish of the Resurrection dissolved. In 2009, the parish of St Luke became separate again.

1. *Brighton Daily Gazette & Sussex Telegraph,* Friday, April 17, 1885
2. Ibid.
3. Phelps, 1974

The building (later destroyed by fire) was originally made as a chapel of ease. There is a modern block of flats on the site, which stands opposite St Luke's Church. *(James Gray Collection, the photographic archive of The Regency Society; with kind permission)*

Inside St Luke's Church

In his 1974 guide, the Revd Phelps says the interior 'really consists of three rooms': the nave, the chancel and, to the south east, the Lady Chapel.

The windows in the north aisle contain six stained glass figures – the Prophetess Anna, Prophet Simeon, and St James, St Andrew, St Peter, St John.

The south aisle windows are now plain, a 1967 replacement of the original stained glass, to allow sunlight to enter, giving a sense of space.

The Lady Chapel windows include the Virgin Mary with the Child Jesus, St Luke with his symbol the winged ox, St John with his symbol the eagle. They were donated in 1901 and made by Charles Eamer Kempe (1837-1907), a well-known Victorian stained glass designer and manufacturer whose work can be seen in English cathedrals.

The Caen stone pulpit with polished columns bears a carved representation of St Luke's ox. The reredos consists of five paintings – Christ in the centre flanked by four Angels in the style of Early Italian Renaissance painter, Fra Angelico. The Angel panels were restored by parish donations in 2010.

The organ, installed in October 1885 by Henry Bevington and Sons of Soho, London, at a cost of £500, is considered one of the finest examples of its kind. Today, few Bevington organs have survived untouched but the one in St Luke's has remained as built except for the addition, in 1992 when the organ was fully restored, of two incomplete stops intended as part of the original specification.

Local man and 1930s choirboy Ken Chambers, writing in his memoirs spanning 1929-1943, recalls pumping the organ bellows by hand: 'quite a strenuous task … The bellows were hand operated by means

Interior of Lady Chapel, St Luke's Church

of a large wooden beam, which protruded from the back of the organ, and had to be constantly moved up and down.'[1]

Ken says it was typical to be fined for misbehaviour, and he had to pay sixpence for talking with his cousin Cyril behind the organ. He also recollects the church was lit by gas 'just sufficient to enable the hymn and prayer books to be read.'[2] The church was gas-lit until 1947 when electric lighting was installed.

In 1986, The Friends of St Luke's Music was set up to raise the funds for the organ restoration; parishioners' funds and donations from others also raised enough to buy a piano. The church could then be used for separate musical concerts so securing its reputation for the quality of its music. Concerts still take place today.

1. Ken Chambers, *Brighton Diaries, Memories of a Young Man in Peace and War 1929-1943* (Hanover Books, 2009)
2. Ibid.

The parish of St Luke's – community; early days

When the new church was being built, the parish of St Luke's – established in 1880 – was one of the most impoverished in Brighton and it was shaping its identity as a community. During the 1800s Brighton was expanding, with better transport connections, and by 1901 the population rose to over 123,000.

In 1871, the major occupation for women was lodging house keeper, followed by domestic servant and laundry worker.[1] For men, there was work on the railways and in the breweries, coal merchants, builders, and the newly-formed electricity and gas industries.

Many of St Luke's male parishioners worked in the building trade and were often laid off. The Revd Firth, first vicar of St Luke's, mentions the area's poverty: 'The hardest and most incessant work in the parish has been the temporal care of the sick and needy, and during many severe winter seasons, the unemployed.'[2]

According to the Revd Phelps' 1974 history, St Luke's in the 1880s was offering charitable, educational, self-help, and social clubs including the Brass Band; Band of Hope, a national temperance movement concerned by the effects of people's excessive drinking and cruelty on children; Coal and Clothing Club – again, it was a national self-help movement popular in poorer areas; Mothers' Meeting, which would become the Mothers' Union into the 1970s; Children's Class; Temperance Society; Dorcas Society, a national network to provide clothing for the poor.

Also, the Choral Society; Cricket Club; Boys' Brigade; St Agnes' Guild for Girls; Lending Library; Penny Bank; Girls' Friendly Society, a society begun in 1875 to help in Christian values young, unmarried women who had become pregnant; a support group for young, single women; a Girls' Guild; Sunday Schools; Missionary Association; Mothers' Guild; Debating Society; a Young Man's Club. The mission statement on the church's website today is: 'A Place for People at the Heart of the Queen's Park Community.'[3] Since it was built, it has always played a central role in the area's social and spiritual life.

Baptism records

Rising house prices have brought changes, and twenty-first century baptism records show parents' work previously listed as tram conductor, shop assistant, factory workers now also include chief executive, company director, university lecturer. The social pattern of people of the parish is diverse.

THE CHURCH OF ST. LUKE.—The contract for this noble building is on the eve of completion. The occasion has been celebrated by a special Thanksgiving Service in the School-Church, a supper as well as a book being given to the workmen employed. We have much pleasure in testifying here to the substantial character of the work carried out by Messrs. Goddard & Son, under the supervision of Mr. Llewellyn, the diligent and kindly Clerk of the works.

PRESENTATION.—At the recent meeting of the Guild of St. Luke a magnificent banner was presented to the members by Miss Gorham, to be first used on the occasion of the opening of the permanent Church. The emblem representing St. Luke (Rev. iv. 7) is beautifully worked upon the centre of the banner.

THE GRAND TEMPERANCE DEMONSTRATION.—On the August Bank Holiday this year, Withdeane was again the scene of a great Demonstration and our own Temperance Society, both adult and juvenile, took part in it. After morning Service we assembled outside the School-Church and marched to the general *rendezvous* in the centre of the Town. With our flags and banners we looked sufficiently gay: and by the aid of our Drum and Fife Band, under the Deputy Bandmaster Walker, we were enlivened and supported during the course of the long processions and at intervals during the day. The day was thoroughly enjoyable and the effect of the Demonstration upon the Town generally cannot but be wholesome and we hope lasting.

At our next monthly meeting, Wednesday, September, 5th, the address will be given by Rev. S. G. Scott, Rector of Woolwich, and one of the foremost Temperance Advocates of our day. We hope there will be a good attendance.

OUR COAL CLUB.—As last year, we are unwilling to go out of our District for a supply of the Coal we require. Any coal merchant in St. Luke's District who is willing to compete for the required supply should send in his tender with particulars to the Vicar-Designate on or before September 15th. The coal will need to be delivered in the month of December. More than one tender will probably be accepted and each subscriber allowed to choose between them.

Detail of *St Luke's Parish Magazine*, September 1883

1. Rose Collis, *The New Encyclopaedia of Brighton* (Brighton and Hove Libraries, 2010)
2. The Revd Firth, *parish magazine*, 1884
3. www.stlukeschurchbrighton.webeden.co.uk

Flint contains the reminder of parishioners who built the boundary around St Luke's parish in the 1880s. A rare plant grows from the flint of the church.

Parishioners in the 1880s

In the 1880s – many years before the welfare state – communities would look after their own, and there was a tradition of churches providing material, financial and spiritual help. The St Luke's Penny Bank, established in 1883, helped local people to manage their money. The Revd Firth administered transactions from a ledger, which is available in the East Sussex Records Office.[1] Parishioners would deposit small sums they could withdraw soon afterwards.

The parish magazine of September 1883 gives a snapshot of the church's early days and the role it played in its parishioners' lives. Listed in the staff are not only 'Vicar-Designate, Rev. W. A. Firth' but others including a 'Mission Lady, Miss Andrewes' and 'District Nurse, Miss L. Broadbridge, 82, London Road.'[2]

The church constantly eased the burden of its impoverished community. The Revd Firth helped the sick by writing letters to qualify parishioners for free outpatient medical assistance with fees paid out of a church fund.

In February 1884, 400 children were offered warm clothing and books at a Sunday School Treat. That year's New Year's Eve dinner provided a meal for 90 adults followed by a tea party for children when 'every child received a useful present'. Without this initiative, 'the appalling conditions of the unemployed would have been unbearable.'[3] 1885 was one of the worst years for the poor in Brighton's history. In February 1885, the Revd Firth had set up an appeal for donations to provide free soup dinners to families of the unemployed. In March, the vicar resorted to providing work for 70-80 local men, employing them on building works in return for food.

The men worked each day for about seven hours: 'The work has been to excavate and build boundary walls round the church and parsonage sites.'[4] Walls bear reminders of the past. In the next century, the Revd Phelps would note it was from such tough conditions that St Luke's church and parish emerged.

The church and the vicarage are solid evidence 'of the days when only Fr Firth and his parish workers stood between whole families and starvation.'[5]

1. Documents – St Luke's Penny Bank; St Luke's Youth Fellowship; St Luke's Queen's Park Young Wives' Group; 1883-1965; East Sussex Records Office
2. *St Luke's parish magazine*, September 1883
3. Phelps, 1974
4. The Revd Firth, *parish magazine*, 1885
5. Phelps, 1974

Fundraising innovations

St Luke's was always at the forefront of fundraising for the church and others – and to trying out new ideas.

In April 1891, *The Argus* newspaper published an article by a journalist who reports on the preparations for a rag fair after going to visit its organiser, 'the energetic lay-reader' of St Luke's, Mr Streeter.[1]

Declaring himself as 'the originator of rag fairs in Brighton, having seen a stall of jumble for sale in a corner of a flower shop on a choir trip to Portsmouth', he had hit on a way to raise funds.

The Argus reporter follows Mr Streeter 'up a steep ladder into the loft over the Vestry' and describes articles collected for the fair. 'Bursting bedding, decrepit mattresses, mildewed boots, bits of fringy stuff, which the representative was informed was carpet.'

The reporter quotes Mr Streeter: 'To give you an illustration on one occasion I counted four hundred persons enter the sale in one hour. That sale realised between £30 and £40.'

Mr Streeter – who appealed by letter in *The Argus* for items to sell[2] – was on the right track. Rag sales or "jumble sales" have been a popular part of fundraising through the twentieth century and into the present, with a brief gap during the Second World War as people had run out of things to sell.

Original ticket from church fundraising event

RAG FAIR AT ST. LUKE'S: BRIGHTON.

An extraordinary collection of second-hand articles of every description was opened yesterday for public inspection, and for sale at very low prices, in the St. Luke's Schoolroom, Islingword-road, Brighton. "Rag fairs," however, are no novelty in that part of Brighton. Many such have been held in connection with St. Luke's, and have proved a great blessing to many poor inhabitants of a populous district. In fact one of the most successful ever held took place no longer ago than last November, when Mr. C. H. Streeter had the satisfaction of handing over a considerable sum to the charities connected with the church as the result. Yesterday's sale promised no less, for during the three hours of the afternoon so busy a trade prevailed that some £20 found its way into the treasury. The "fair" is laid out rather for utility than ornament; there are a few benches round the room, and on these are arranged heaps of articles of various descriptions. On one bench, for instance, are dozens of pairs of boots ranging from well-worn Wellingtons down to soiled satin slippers. The average price of these seems to be about 9d. At another stall one can get for 6d. a top hat that once was fit for a prince, and now might very easily be made almost equal to new. In the centre of the room are one or two bedsteads, which, if not priced quite so low, are at least within the selling value as firewood. There is a stall of books, a pile of music, a number of clocks, most of them with "something wrong with the works" of course; there are garments of all descriptions, and many times during the day Mr. Streeter, who is chief salesman, cashier, everything that one man possibly can be, was appealed to for something that would do for "our Joe:" there are vases, scrubbing brushes, photographs, and pictures, china ornaments, and oddities of all descriptions, in hundreds and thousands. They were no doubt diminished in number by yesterday's rush, but Mr. Streeter will probably produce from some secret place quite a large enough assortment to fill up the room of those taken away. That these "rag fairs" are appreciated was evident from the crowd that had collected outside the door long before the time for opening arrived, a crowd that meant business too, for every person on entering was required to hand over threepence, "not to be returned in goods." Among those assisting Mr. Streeter yesterday, and who, as stated, were kept pretty well employed throughout the afternoon and evening, were Miss Allum, Miss Burrell, Miss Baker, Miss Burgh, Mrs. Firth, Rev. E. J. Frayling, Mrs. Gray, Mr. Hawker, Mrs. Jones, Miss Kay, Mr. Luff, Mrs. Morant, Miss Newman, Mrs. Streeter, Mr. C. R. Streeter, jun., Mr. Scott, and Mrs Short. The "rag fair" opens again to-day from three till six and from seven till ten.

Account of the rag fair, St Luke's, April 29, 1891 (courtesy of *The Argus*)

1. *The Argus*, April 18, 1891
2. *The Argus*, April 14, 1891

The church and the community during the World Wars

In common with people throughout the country, the congregation of St Luke's raised funds to help war efforts. Along with other parishes, the church had its share of heartache and loss.

One of the fallen of the First World War was Lt Robert Percival Young of the 1st/4th Bn Royal Sussex Regiment, killed in Palestine in 1917, the only child of St Luke's vicar, the Revd A J Young. An oak memorial in St Luke's is dedicated to Lt Young and other 'parishioners who made the supreme sacrifice.'[1]

As that conflict drew to a close, St Luke's marked its gratitude to the people whose struggle ended the war. The Vestry Minutes, April 22, 1919, propose the congregation 'extend a hearty welcome to the soldiers and sailors who have returned from the perils of the "Great War", in the form of a tea and concert.'[2]

The Second World War saw the church pulling together with the rest of the community. The Revd Barnett gave permission to the local authority to use the church hall as an emergency clearing centre for casualties and offered the vicarage room as a place for children outside school hours. Gifts were sent to the men of the parish on active service.

In 1942, a parcel was sent to Fred Sadler, a local man being held prisoner of war. Mr Sadler wrote back requesting a photo of the interior of the church, which was duly dispatched to him.

St Luke's parish did not escape bombing. In May 1943, two pupils at St Luke's School, Billy Eatwell and eight-year-old David Bell – a choirboy of the church – were killed in a sweetshop on Down Terrace. Bombs were dropped on Albion Hill and nearby Lewes Road Inn.[3]

Oak memorial to Lt Young, St Luke's

The names of local parishioners who died in wartime service are shown on the memorial boards in the church. The end of the Second World War was marked by a Garden Fete and a Harvest Festival; offerings were donated to the Queen's Nurses.

1. Special Vestry Meeting Minutes, September 23, 1918
2. Vestry Minutes, April 22, 1919
3. *School Reports: Past Pupils' Memories of St Luke's*

Exterior, St Luke's Church

Chancel and Lady Chapel, St Luke's

The church from the 1950s

The 1950s started with a shock when it was reported St Luke's was going to be demolished and the parish merged with other churches. However, 200 parishioners met and unanimously voted against the move. For the next two years the church worked to increase its income – and be less vulnerable – through fundraising events and door-to-door collections. The church could pay its way by 1952 and was safe.

The church's clubs and associations were still going strong but showing a change in focus. Reflecting a more equal society with the resources of the welfare state, such things as the Coal and Clothing Club were no more. The parish reports on talks by local people such as a butcher, a female magistrate, a vicar from Shoreham, and in 1969 a talk on a new wonder substance – formica.

The Men's Group was another long-running group, in existence since 1904 and meeting in the Bute Hall on Sutherland Road, which is now a carpet shop. The parish magazines from the late 1960s also show a programme for the Mothers' Union Group and a Junior Youth Fellowship.

The church was still active in raising funds for others and at the end of 1969 the Young Wives' Group, which folded the following year, generated money to distribute between elderly people in time for Christmas. The parish magazines of the 1960s give the impression of a friendly and generous congregation. Now in 2015, people show a similar commitment to fundraising and gratitude for the legacy of music.

As well as The Friends of St Luke's Music, the well-established church choir continues its music tradition and sings at other churches and cathedrals in Britain. In 2010, another chapter of history was created. The Revd Julie Newson became St Luke's first woman incumbent, steering the church in philanthropy, interaction, diversity and welcome.

She encourages parishioners to support charitable initiatives such as a food bank and to develop the church's facilities opening up a community space for groups such as Line Dancing; Sun Power Yoga; Crafty Kids Cook Club; Soup 'n' Sarnie; Pilates, Music Makers.

St Luke's parish: Brighton General Hospital and the workhouse[1]

Brighton General Hospital began as the town's Elm Grove workhouse in 1865 with building by George Maynard. It opened in September 1867 when 529 'paupers' – maintained by the parish – walked up the hill to Elm Grove. Brighton workhouse was one of the largest institutions in the country.

On admission to the workhouse people were examined, washed, required to surrender possessions, given a uniform, allocated a ward. The regime was hard and families were separated. Once in the workhouse, it was difficult to leave.

Inmates who died at the workhouse were buried at the extramural cemetery in Lewes Road. In 1878 it was found that, to save money, names were chalked onto coffins, only to be erased if it rained.

In pre-NHS days, if people were unable to pay for medical attention, they could also be admitted to the workhouse upon the signature of a medical officer.

In May 1914, the dropping of the term workhouse for poor law institutions reflected a more compassionate attitude. The inmate was changing to a person who may require medical attention, heralding the development of the premises into a hospital but before this the First World War intervened. The War Office notified it needed the premises as a hospital for volunteer troops from India.

Brighton Poor Law Institution in 1921 reverted back; the Elm Grove building was reoccupied by its inmates. During the 1920s, the hospital side began to develop, with the infirmary approved in 1922 as a training school for nurses.

In the run-up to the Second World War, air raid sirens were placed in the building, basements adapted for shelters and sandbags procured. When war was declared, wards were taken over as an Air Raid Precaution – ARP – first aid post. The main building was evacuated to deal with emergency cases and to accommodate patients from hospitals in vulnerable areas. In 1948, after the National Insurance Act of 1946, the NHS renamed the facility Brighton General Hospital. Local man Roy Devereux, a paperboy to the hospital during 1940, recalls when he was eight years old.

Roy saw men queuing up at the hospital for a bed for the night. A reception centre for homeless people operated there into the 1970s.

Men laying tram tracks by the old workhouse building, Elm Grove, Brighton (*James Gray Collection, the photographic archive of The Regency Society; with kind permission*)

Foundation stone, Elm Grove workhouse, 1865

1. Source material: James Gardner, *A History of Brighton Workhouses* (Brighton, 2012)

Around the parish: Brighton home for female penitents[1]

In 1868, property was acquired on Finsbury Road to house 'female penitents'. An earlier survey recorded over 300 'fallen women' and measures were taken to facilitate their reform. In 1853, the Revd George Wagner set up the first home for the rehabilitation of women, which was taken over in 1857 by a convent of Anglican nuns – founded by George's cousin, the Revd Arthur Wagner. The facility was re-named St Mary's Home for Penitent Women and as need increased, part of the institution was moved to Egremont Place. The 1868 property on Finsbury Road was opened as a branch – known as the Albion Hill Home – where women could be sent by clergy, police, doctors. Some pregnant women turning up at the workhouse would be sent here, and other women sent here were considered 'fallen' if unmarried and having a baby. The regime was tough and women were unable to come and go.
It is likely in the early days babies would have been adopted. By the late 1940s the premises were the Church Army Maternity and Child Welfare Home, converted in the 1950s into a furniture factory, which in 1958 was demolished.

Lewes Road Dispensary (Islingword Road) for women and children

In the past 'dispensaries' were medical institutions that in pre-NHS times offered free or low-cost medical treatment to people unable to afford doctors' fees. The Lewes Road Dispensary for Women and Children, founded by Doctors Helen Boyle and Mabel Jones, opened its doors in October 1899 on Islingword Road. It was a trailblazing establishment, offering services to women and children by an all-female medical staff. In 1899, women had only been able to practise as doctors for a few years and were fighting hard battles in order to do so. The opening of this Dispensary was a radical move. The first page of the Dispensary's 1905 Annual Report, available to see in the Brighton History Centre at The Keep, sets out its aim 'to afford to poor women of Brighton and the neighbourhood, the opportunity of free consultation with Doctors of their own sex.'[2]

Table donation by woman parishioner

1. Archive material: The Keep; Brighton Museums
2. Lewes Road Dispensary for Women and Children Annual Report, 1905, East Sussex Records Office

O'Flinn Pharmacy on Islingword Road, 2015, is now at the centre of the local community's well-being offering a range of free services, advice and support

Around the parish: pioneers

The Dispensary on Islingword Road brought together some of Brighton's most pioneering women. Dr Helen Boyle (1869-1957) was Brighton's first female GP, the first female psychiatrist at the Royal Sussex County Hospital, and co-founder of MIND. Born in Dublin, she arrived in Brighton in 1897 after working in London's East End, gaining first-hand knowledge of the ways living in poverty could take its mental and physical toll on poor women. Her aim was to transform the treatment of working-class women with early-stage mental illness, whom she fiercely defended and described as 'neglected and maltreated'. *(www.brightonmuseums.org.uk)*

Dr Louisa Martindale (1872-1966), another early female GP, was a visiting medical officer at the Dispensary. She was instrumental in the setting up of the New Sussex Hospital for Women on Windlesham Road, and held the post of senior surgeon and physician until 1937. She became a pioneer in the early treatment of cervical cancer by X-ray. She served in France during the First World War and was a surgeon in London in the Second World War.

Elizabeth Garrett-Anderson (1812-1903) was the Dispensary's Vice-President. In 1866, she had established a Dispensary for Women in London and was later made a visiting physician at the East London Hospital for Children – the first woman in Britain to be appointed to a medical post. In 1874, she co-established the London School of Medicine for Women. The Dispensary was replaced by a hospital on Round Hill Crescent in 1905.

Mercedes Gleitze, famous swimmer

According to Helena Wojtczak, author of *Notable Sussex Women: 280 Biographical Sketches*, 124 Freshfield Road was the birthplace of Mercedes Gleitze (1900-1981), a woman who achieved incredible swimming feats. A bilingual secretary in her day job, on 7 October 1927 Mercedes became the first British woman to swim the English Channel. In 1928, she was the first person to swim the Straits of Gibraltar from Tarifa in southern Spain to Morocco. In May 1933, she broke the British endurance swimming record when she swam for 47 hours in Worthing baths. She became a celebrity and spent her fortune on charitable causes helping people in distress.

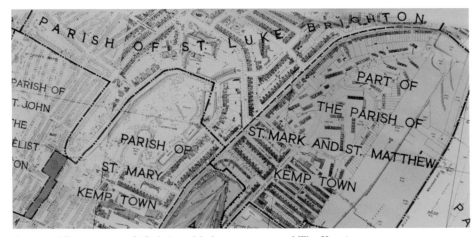

Feature of Deanery map, St Luke's parish (image courtesy of The Keep)

Listed building, Pepper Pot – opposite St Luke's Church

Detail of garden temple, originally part of Thomas Attree's villa

Children in Queen's Park, early 1900s, close to St Luke's School and to the church *(James Gray Collection, the photographic archive of The Regency Society; with kind permission)*

Education in the parish: St Luke's School

St Luke's School was built in 1903 by Thomas Simpson, architect of the Brighton and Preston School Board, in reaction to the Elementary Education Act 1870 that required local councils to create provision for universal elementary education. Responding to the poor conditions of schools in the area and Brighton's fast-growing population, St Luke's School was the final one of several built for the Board by Simpson. It has been referred to as 'the culmination of his career'. In 2003, to celebrate the school's centenary, a book was produced – an oral history based on interviews.[1] In 2009, the Infants and Junior School joined together and became known as St Luke's Primary School.

Landmarks in the parish: Pepper Pot, garden temple

An historic structure opposite the church is the Pepper Pot, a Grade II listed building since 1952. It was built in 1830 by famed architect Sir Charles Barry (1795-1860) in the grounds of a villa to his design and belonging to Thomas Attree (1778-1863) who bought Queen's Park in 1825. After Thomas Attree's death, the villa and park were owned by George Duddell who set up Tower Press in the Pepper Pot where he produced a daily newspaper, *The Brighton Mail*. Despite having Grade II listed status, the villa was demolished in 1972 after serving as the Xaverian Roman Catholic College from 1909-1966. The remaining elements of Attree's villa is a garden temple – an Italianate structure with Ionic pillars in the grounds of Carn Court flats. Dawn Grenville, company secretary of Carn Court Residents' Association Ltd, explains in April 2013's *Queens Park Living* that the structure was falling into such disrepair the residents wholly funded the restoration in 2012 at a cost of £22,000.

1. Project Co-ordinator Jackie Blackwell, *School Reports: Past Pupils' Memories of St Luke's* (QueenSpark Books, 2003)

Artist Lisa Holdcroft depicts the local parish and draws together church, Royal Mail van, number 18 bus and shelter, people, church warden, Pepper Pot, trees, dog, seagull

Writing from the St Luke's prayer and poetry event outside with passersby beside the Pepper Pot bus stop

Operated by Brighton & Hove Bus and Coach Company, the number 18 stops at the Pepper Pot bus stop – a vital transport link for the community

St Luke's popular vicarage dog, Delilah

A swift by the tower nest in St Luke's Church. Image courtesy of Chris Lowe – historic and wildlife conservation

The Post Office with shop on Islingword Road is a renowned meeting point of the local parish where staff give a warm welcome

Grocery store STOCK on Islingword Place has full shelves, to provide its supplies to the local community

Heart of the community: local church, local businesses, local bus stop

In the past many shops and businesses operated locally, giving people the chance to earn their livelihoods and obtain everything they needed on their doorstep. Some of the establishments have been turned into houses yet showing a resemblance to their past such as a shop, a pub or a chapel. Today the parish of St Luke's covers a mainly residential area. Community services that remain include the Post Office, O'Flinn the pharmacy, a medical centre, and STOCK, the specialty grocery store. A key local transport link is the bus service, which brings together the community. The vicarage, close by, is first point of call for groups that wish to access the community space in the church.